For Lucy I, Val C and Julia G   N. D.

For Will and his generosity   N. L.

First published 2007 by Walker Books Ltd, 87 Vauxhall Walk, London SE11 5HJ

10 9 8 7 6 5 4 3 2 1

Text © 2007 Nicola Davies   Illustrations © 2007 Neal Layton

The right of Nicola Davies and Neal Layton to be identified as author and illustrator respectively of this work has been asserted by them in accordance with the Copyright, Designs and Patents Act 1988

This book has been typeset in AT Arta

Printed in Singapore

British Library Cataloguing in Publication Data: a catalogue record for this book is available from the British Library

ISBN 978-1-4063-0095-6

www.walkerbooks.co.uk

THE CHIMPANZEE ON THE OPPOSITE PAGE IS ABOUT TO EAT A **BIG** BUNCH OF SPIKY LEAVES. YOU CAN FIND OUT WHY IF YOU TURN TO PAGE 46...

What's Eating You?

Parasites – the Inside Story

by **Nicola Davies**

illustrated by **Neal Layton**

GULP!

WALKER BOOKS
AND SUBSIDIARIES
LONDON · BOSTON · SYDNEY · AUCKLAND

Up a tree or down a hole,

out to sea or in a puddle,

somewhere hot or somewhere cold ...

every animal has a habitat, a place where it belongs,
a place where it can find food and shelter and have its babies.

You Are a Habitat!

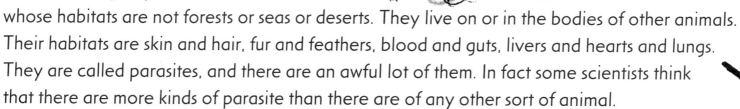

But there is a group of creatures whose habitats are not forests or seas or deserts. They live on or in the bodies of other animals. Their habitats are skin and hair, fur and feathers, blood and guts, livers and hearts and lungs. They are called parasites, and there are an awful lot of them. In fact some scientists think that there are more kinds of parasite than there are of any other sort of animal.

Almost every free-living animal on the planet is just a walking habitat – a "host" to many parasites – and that includes us humans! There are more than 430 different kinds of parasite that can live on a human body (ectoparasites) or in one (endoparasites).

Don't panic! Modern humans are too clean and well cared for to have lots of parasites. You certainly don't have 430 different kinds! But you may just have one or two, even if you think you don't. That's because although some parasites make their hosts feel rather ill, others don't do any harm at all and you would never know you were being used as a habitat. But you *mite* find out about those later! (There's a clue there. Just wait and see.)

Meet Some Ectoparasites...

(They live on the outside of bodies.)

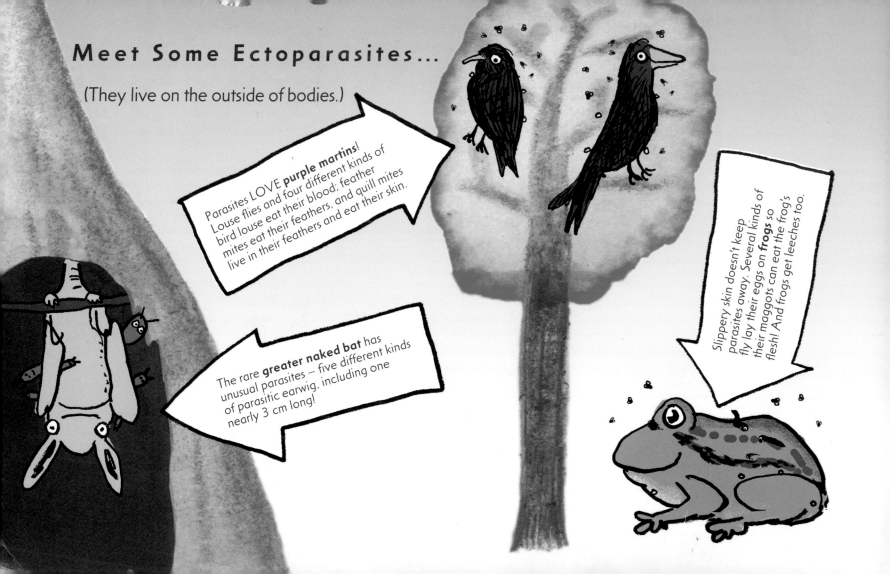

Parasites LOVE **purple martins**! Louse flies and four different kinds of bird louse eat their blood; feather mites eat their feathers, and quill mites live in their feathers and eat their skin.

The rare **greater naked bat** has five different kinds of unusual parasites — including one of parasitic earwig, nearly 3 cm long!

Slippery skin doesn't keep parasites away. Several kinds of fly lay their eggs on **frogs** so their maggots can eat the frog's flesh! And frogs get leeches too.

Humans probably don't have more parasites than other animals, but scientists have studied us the most, and found lots: head lice, body lice, fleas...

Dogs can have two kinds of fleas and lice, three kinds of mite and as many as six kinds of tick living on their skin and fur.

Moles have the biggest fleas in the world, up to 8 mm long.

Copepods are relatives of shrimps and parasites of **blue sharks**. There's a copepod parasite in all these places: the pectoral fins, the nostrils, the gills. Oh, yes ... and they have leeches too!

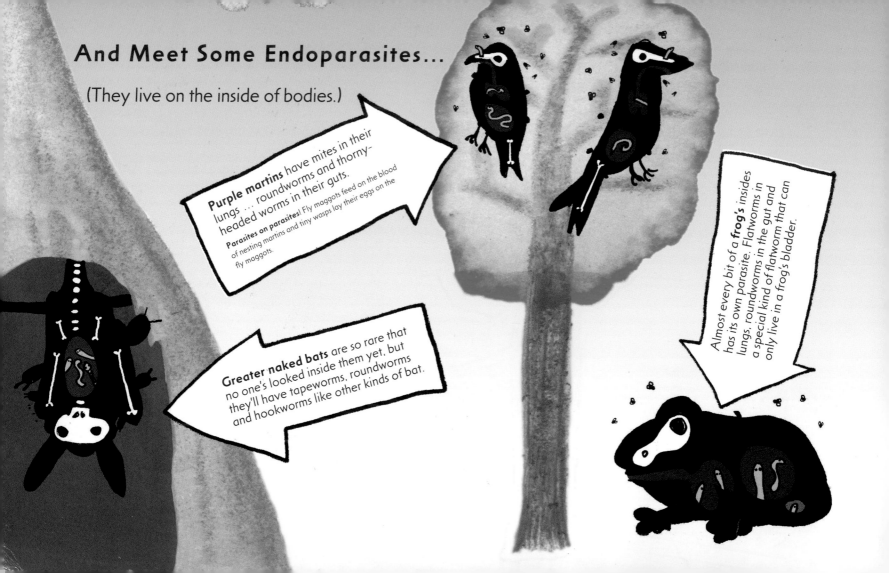

And Meet Some Endoparasites...

(They live on the inside of bodies.)

Purple martins have mites in their lungs ... roundworms and thorny-headed worms in their guts.

Parasites on parasites! Fly maggots feed on the blood of nesting martins and tiny wasps lay their eggs on the fly maggots.

Greater naked bats are so rare that no one's looked inside them yet, but they'll have tapeworms, roundworms and hookworms like other kinds of bat.

Almost every bit of a **frog's** insides has its own parasite. Flatworms in lungs, roundworms in the gut and a special kind of flatworm that can only live in a frog's bladder.

What Makes a Good Parasite?

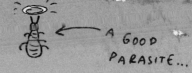

A GOOD PARASITE...

Polar bears need thick coats to beat the cold, and giraffes need long necks to reach their food. But parasites need to be much cleverer than ordinary animals to survive in their body-habitats.

First, they need to be small; it's no good being the size of an elephant if your habitat is the fur of a mouse. And second, they need to be super-adaptable, because finding a host can be very different from living on it or in it; being able to change body shape is a big advantage to a parasite.

THE PARASITE CLUB

MEMBERS ONLY NO MAMMALS OR BIG FISH

Most vertebrates — birds, mammals, reptiles, amphibians and fish — can't be parasites; they're just too big. Also, their bodies are set in one form. But invertebrate animals like insects, worms, snails and single-celled animals are small and can change their body shape and form during their lives (think of caterpillars turning into butterflies). So some of them make really good parasites and can adapt to life on and off their chosen host in mind-bogglingly amazing ways.

Getting Aboard

Living bodies are not the easiest places to live. They do things that other habitats don't do. For a start they move about, so the first problem a parasite has to solve is how to get onto its habitat and stay there. Which, as most hosts are much bigger and faster than their parasites, can seem as impossible as a mouse trying to hitch a ride on a jumbo jet. Yet parasites manage it all the time.

The most basic approach to host-hitching is to hang around and hope that one will pass by. This is what ticks do. These little blood-sucking relatives of spiders only stay on their hosts long enough to get a meal. They climb into grass and bushes, and when they smell that an animal is close, they wave their legs to grab a ride.

This "hit 'n' miss" method often works, because ticks aren't picky eaters – any warm-blooded animal will do, humans included – and they don't need to hang on for long. As soon as they've had their blood meal, and swollen from full-stop to fat-baked-bean size, they drop off, back to the grass to lay eggs.

Most fleas don't live on their host full-time either. They start life as larvae, living in their host's bed. When the adult fleas hatch they rely on warmth or movement to tell them there's a body nearby, and then they start leaping ... and leaping ... and leaping. They can keep leaping for hours on end – jumping up to one hundred times their own body length, which is like a man jumping over the Eiffel Tower! With luck, this will bring the flea into contact with a host. Then it can grab ahold and wriggle down in the jungle of fur or feathers. If anything tries to pull it out, the flea is covered in backwards-pointing spines that tangle in the host's coat and hold it fast.

AFTER ALL THAT, I'M STAYING PUT!

19

There are lots of kinds of flea, and they all have a favourite host. But the "big leap" method of host-finding is a bit unreliable (you can't be sure what you'll jump onto), so most fleas are able to get a meal from more than one kind of animal. Cat fleas, for example, find humans quite tasty, and human fleas will bite dogs, pigs and even burrowing owls!

WANTED TASTY HOST
HUNGRY FLEA SEEKS A HOST.
NOT FUSSY.
ANY CAT, PIG OR BURROWING OWL WILL DO.

Staying Aboard

One way to avoid getting on the wrong host is never to get off the right one. Parasites that do this have to become experts at living on one kind of host – so good, in fact, that they can't live anywhere else.

Rabbit fleas never leave their bunny hosts; they even breed at the same time as their bunnies. When baby rabbits are born, the fleas move from mum to babies. They lay their eggs on the babies, then move back to mum. But newly hatched flea grubs can't suck blood, so before the adult fleas return to mother rabbit, they make food for their offspring – a load of their own poo, specially rich in bunny blood, for the grubs to munch on. This way adults and young fleas get everything they need aboard their rabbit world.

Human hair mites get all they need from their hosts – us! They are diddy relatives of spiders, about one tenth of millimetre long (less than the size of a grain of salt), with bodies like miniature salamis and four

pairs of stumpy legs. They live in the roots of hair (usually eyelashes or eyebrows), where they munch on dead skin and sebum (the oily stuff that keeps hair shiny). The only time they wander is when young mites search for a hair of their own, when they may find their way onto another body.

You *might* have mites without knowing. (Remember that clue?) Your granny almost certainly does, because your chances of getting mites go up with age. But don't worry, they're harmless.

A SUPER-ENLARGED DRAWING OF A HUMAN HAIR MITE

0.1 mm
(WHICH IS REALLY, REALLY, REALLY SMALL)

DEAD SKIN AND SEBUM! MY FAVOURITE!

COME AND GIVE YOUR GRANDMA AND HER HAIR MITES A BIG CUDDLE! EH?

23

Lice: the Stay-at-Home Specialists

You certainly would know about it if you had lice. Their bites would make your skin itch, and if you had a lot of lice, you might even feel tired and sick, "lousy" in fact.

Human head lice, otherwise known as "cooties", are so brilliant at living on our hair that they can't live anywhere else. They are tiny (less than 1.5 mm), so they can hide easily, and they have claws exactly the right size to grab human head hair. They are incredibly tough and can survive hair-washing with no difficulty at all. Even if you manage to wash out the grown-ups, the eggs (commonly called "nits") survive.

The stay-at-home tactics of lice have let them specialize in living on one type of host or even one bit of a host. There are lice that only live on birds' *wings* and others that only live on their *heads*; there are lice that only live on guinea pigs and lice that only live on seals. In fact, lice have been so successful that there are 3000 different kinds.

The Louse Family

Legless, Eyeless, Mouthless ... and Ready!

Parasites that live on the inside of bodies — endoparasites — are more specialized than the most stay-at-home louse. They may not have legs, eyes, or even mouths and guts, because inside a body they don't need them. So endoparasites can look seriously weird.

The human tapeworm, for instance, looks like a visitor from another planet. Tapeworms can live in your intestine, and grow to 20 m long! Their bodies are shaped like a tape measure, and made of hundreds of little flattened segments. Instead of a head they have a thing called a scolex, a kind of knob with a series of hooks and suckers on it, that holds onto the inside of the intestine. They don't have eyes, because there's no light to see with in an intestine, and they don't have legs, because they don't go anywhere. They don't need a mouth or a gut of their own, because they just float around in your digested food and soak it up through their skin.

There are plenty of other wormy parasites that can live in your guts: whipworms, like bits of spaghetti; roundworms, big as your finger, and tiny thread-like pinworms — all bathing in your food. And there are hookworms, which don't feed on your *food*, but feed on *you*, munching intestines and blood.

SCOLEX

5 m   10 m

TAPEWORM   TAPE MEASURE

Sneaking in

The question is, how do these animals get into your intestine? Obviously you'd notice if you were swallowing a twenty-metre tapeworm, or even a couple of little pinworms. This is where the common invertebrate trick of morphing from one body form to another comes in handy for parasites. They get into your body as teeny eggs or larvae, and then change into their grown-up selves!

Pinworms, for example, get into you as eggs. The adult worm pokes out of its host's bottom at night to lay eggs on the skin just outside. The eggs are so tiny and light that they can just blow all over a house, and into mouths, without anyone noticing. Once the pinworm eggs get swallowed, they hatch out when they reach the gut.

Hookworm eggs are squeezed out with their host's poo, but because humans don't eat their own poo (some animals do — rabbits, for instance!), hookworms need some other route into a new body. So ... the eggs hatch into baby hookworms tiny enough to wiggle between human skin cells and, in places where poo can be stepped in by people, they get into the blood and then back to the gut — where they grow up and start feeding.

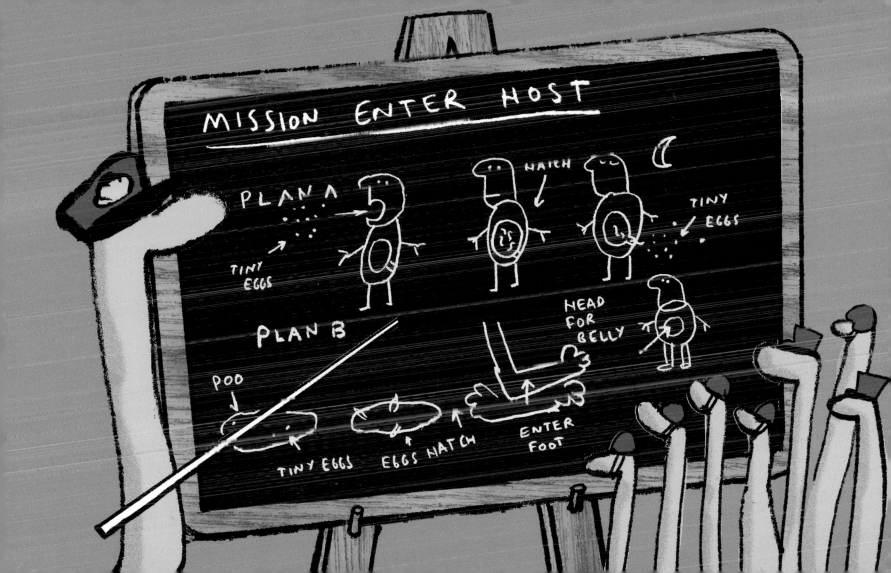

START

Roll a 1 to start.

YOU ARE AN ~~EGG~~ EGG POOED OUT IN A PERSON'S POO...

ROLL A 1 OR 2 TO CONTINUE.

THE POO IS FLUSHED AWAY. GO BACK TO START.

THE POO ENDS UP in a field. MOVE ON ONE SQUARE.

YOU

HATCH INTO AN ADULT TAPEWORM AND LAY THOUSANDS OF EGGS.

THE Two-host Tapeworm GAME

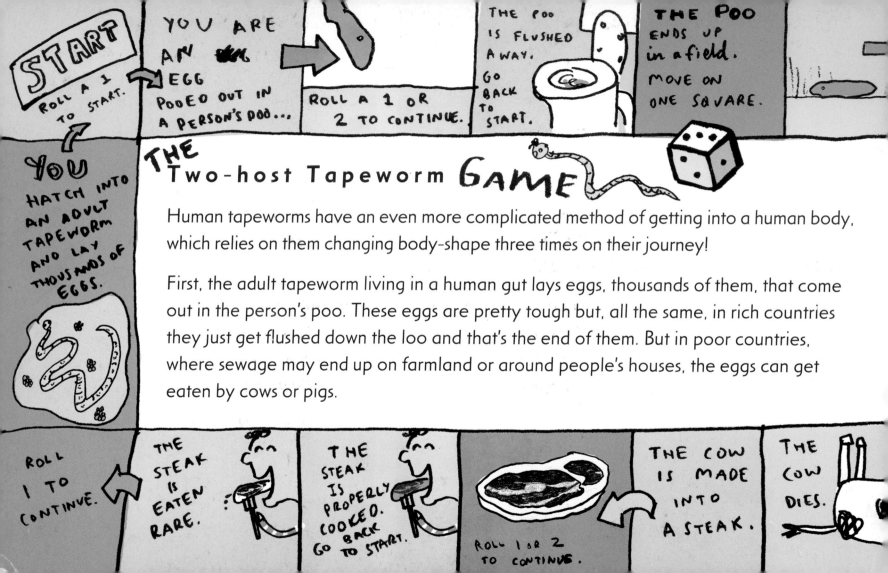

Human tapeworms have an even more complicated method of getting into a human body, which relies on them changing body-shape three times on their journey!

First, the adult tapeworm living in a human gut lays eggs, thousands of them, that come out in the person's poo. These eggs are pretty tough but, all the same, in rich countries they just get flushed down the loo and that's the end of them. But in poor countries, where sewage may end up on farmland or around people's houses, the eggs can get eaten by cows or pigs.

ROLL 1 TO CONTINUE.

THE STEAK IS EATEN RARE.

THE STEAK IS PROPERLY COOKED. GO BACK TO START.

ROLL 1 or 2 TO CONTINUE.

THE COW IS MADE INTO A STEAK.

THE COW DIES.

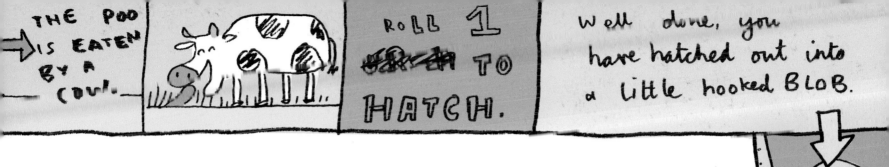

THE POO IS EATEN BY A COW.

ROLL ~~ONE 1 TO~~ 1 TO HATCH.

Well done, you have hatched out into a little hooked BLOB.

Inside a pig or a cow they hatch into little hooked blobs, which wiggle into the blood and ride around until they get to a muscle. There they change again, into an egg-shaped bubble called a bladder worm. (See? Told you it was complicated!)

The tapeworm can't grow up and lay eggs in a cow or a pig. So the bladder worm has to wait … and wait … and wait … until the cow or pig becomes some unlucky person's undercooked beef or pork dinner. The worm slips down with the meal, then pops out of its bubble. Now, at last, it can settle down, turn into an adult and lay eggs.

ROLL A 1 TO FIND A MUSCLE.

MOVE ON ONE SQUARE.

YOU TURN INTO A BLADDER WORM.

Roll a 1 to turn into a bladder worm.

YOU FIND A MUSCLE. GO ON ONE SQUARE.

The Host Is Toast!

Many different kinds of tapeworm use this weird route, getting to the host where they breed (called a "primary host"), via a host where they can't breed (a "secondary host"). This is good news for the primary host, as the tapeworm tries not to hurt it because it wants to stay and breed for as long as possible. But it is very bad news indeed for the secondary host, because the tapeworm wants the secondary host to be eaten as soon as possible. And tapeworms have creepy ways of getting what they want. Let me give you a couple of examples…

32 A tapeworm of herons has a secondary host, which is a little fish called a stickleback. How does it get from fish to heron? By turning the fish orange or white and making it swim so close to the surface of the water that a hunting heron couldn't possibly miss it.

Wolf tapeworms stop off in their secondary host, moose. The tapeworm makes sure it gets to its favourite host – a wolf – by making the moose easy to catch: it gets into the moose's lungs, making its breath smelly and wheezy. So the moose is easy to find and can't run very fast!

And there are many similar stories where the secondary host ends up as the toast of the primary host.

SNIFF ← PRIMARY HOST

SECONDARY HOST PUFF WHEEZE…

Deadly Delivery

Getting eaten seems like a pretty direct route into another animal's body, but there are parasites so small that they can get themselves injected into the blood of their host in the bite of an insect.

If someone asked you what is the most dangerous animal in the world, what would you choose? A tiger? A grizzly bear? A poisonous snake? All wrong. The deadliest creature on the planet — apart from humans of course — is so very small, you'd need a microscope to see it. It's called plasmodium and is delivered in the bite of a mosquito.

34

Millions of plasmodia wait inside a mosquito's mouth until it bites a human. Then they rush down the mozzie's needle-like mouth parts and into the blood. Once in, plasmodia are tiny enough to hide inside a single cell – the body's smallest building block. Each plasmodium makes a cell its slave, using up the cell's energy to make copies of itself, then casting it aside like an empty crisp packet. In two weeks, each plasmodium has made 640,000 copies of itself.

The person with this going on inside is very poorly indeed. They have the disease we call malaria, which kills one million people every year, mostly in warm, wet, tropical countries where mosquitoes are common.

35

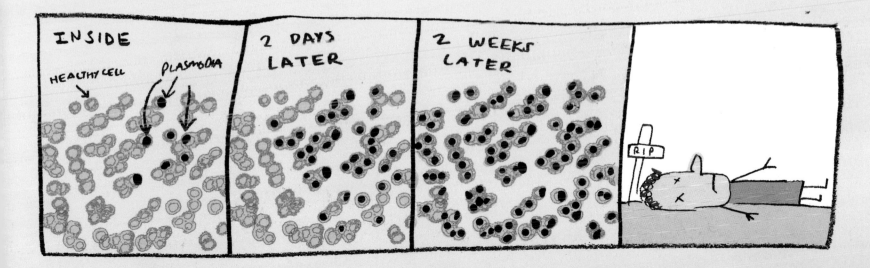

Kill or Cure

As far as the parasite plasmodium is concerned, the host is just a larder. But it must make sure that some of its copies escape before the host dies. So the plasmodium parasites call their mosquito taxi to come and get them by making infected people smell extra nice (actually like cheesy feet!) to mosquitoes. The mozzie bites, sucks up blood with plasmodium parasites in it, then flies off, ready to bite someone else and give the parasite a new host to live in.

36 Where there are lots of people and lots of mosquitoes, this is really easy, so it doesn't matter to the plasmodium if it kills its host – fast. But where getting out to another host could take time – where there are fewer people or mozzies – plasmodium must be kinder and not make its host so ill. The host may even recover from malaria but go on carrying plasmodium parasites in their blood all their life.

← LOTS OF MOZZIES

← NOT SO MANY MOZZIES

Parasite Mind Control

Although plasmodium may make its host very ill (and make them smell like old socks), it doesn't tell the host what to do. But there are plenty of parasites clever enough to control their host as if it was a puppet and the parasite was pulling the strings.

Sacculina is a sea-living relative of crabs. It starts life as a swimming larva, like a tiny shrimp. But as soon as it meets a crab, it shrugs off its whole body, and injects a minute blob of cells into the crab. These grow tentacles into every single part of the crab's body, even its brain, to control everything it does. The crab is now just Sacculina's slave. It eats but doesn't grow, because all its food now feeds Sacculina. It doesn't breed but rears Sacculina's babies instead, as though they were its own. Even male crabs do this: Sacculina makes males behave like females with babies.

Parasitic flies can control bumble-bees' brains and even make them get into their own graves. The flies inject eggs into the bee's body so that the larvae, when they hatch, can eat the bee alive. The larvae want the bee to stay somewhere safe and out of sight so it won't get eaten, so they send a message to the bee's brain. This makes the bee crawl into a hole and cover itself up, before dying.

39

Horsehair worms are parasites that keep their grasshopper hosts healthy until they are ready to return to the water. Then they make the grasshopper want to jump into water, where the worms can break out, leaving the broken body of the grasshopper behind.

Good Grooming Could Save Your Life!

By now you may be feeling rather uncomfortable, even a bit sick, at the thought of parasites using your body as their property. Get ready to feel better. The good news is that there is a lot that we, and other animals, can do to fight back.

Ectoparasites, like ticks, fleas and lice, can weaken an animal and make it easy prey, so good grooming can mean the difference between life and death. Grooming – with teeth and beaks, paws and claws – can do a really good job of combing out and squishing up to 90 per cent of parasites. But it needs to be done regularly – some animals spend up to six hours every day grooming. What's more, many also groom each other to make sure that awkward spots they can't reach themselves are kept parasite-free.

This "I'll scratch your back, if you scratch mine" approach is an important part of animal social life. Grooming the back of your mate's head shows affection in birds. In gorillas, who grooms who is a status symbol, so the top male in the group gets groomed by everyone.

Parasite-popping is so important for kangaroos that they have built-in grooming equipment: two of their toes are stuck together to make a two-clawed grooming tool.

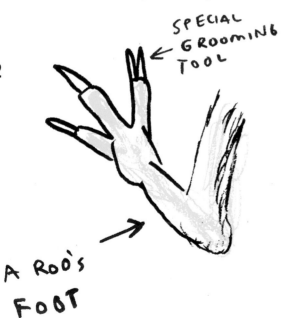

SPECIAL GROOMING TOOL

A ROO'S FOOT

42

A HERON

A HERON'S TOE

Barn owls, and herons, too, have a comb on their middle toe to help scrape lice off their feathers.

Impala tempt ticks into a place where they can get them with their teeth, by having black stripes on their bottoms! Ticks go for warmth, so huddle up in the warm black fur, just where the impala's teeth can reach them.

GOTCHA!

WHIFF!

U STINK!

Starlings use strong-smelling plants in their nests to keep parasites off their babies.

Birds can use chemicals to get rid of parasites. Hoopoes make smelly oil in their preen gland (on the tail) to spread over their feathers and put off parasites. Some jays even pick up ants and use the acid from their stings to kill lice.

PONG!

WARNING

PROPERTY PROTECTED BY VIPER SECURITY!

43

American screech owls, though, may have found the best anti-louse treatment of all: they keep a small insect-eating snake in their nests!

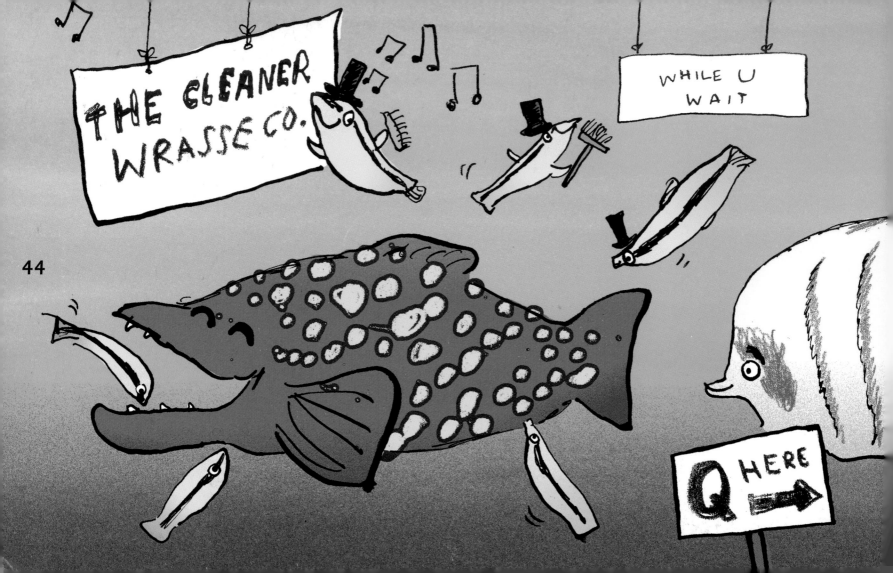

Sea creatures living on tropical reefs can "go to the cleaners" to get rid of parasites. Little striped fish, called cleaner wrasse, specialize in biting the parasites off other fish and turtles. The wrasse show they are ready to do some cleaning by swimming about, wriggling their stripy bodies. Animals with parasites then line up in a queue and wait their turn to be cleaned. The wrasse get a tummy full of juicy parasites as payment for their services!

Breaking the Circle

Medicines aren't always the best way to defeat a parasite. The complicated body-morphing life-cycles of some parasites make them easy to attack using a little bit of knowledge.

Guinea worm is a two-foot-long worm that likes to wander round a human body until it gets to a leg. It makes a hole in the leg which is sore and painful, and the only way the human host can make it feel better is by paddling in cold water. This is just what the guinea worm wants. It releases its tiny babies through the hole into the water, where they get inside the bodies of mini shrimp-type animals called copepods. When a person swallows a copepod in their drinking water, the guinea worm babies leave the shrimp and start their wanderings through another human body all over again.

Three and a half million people, from Africa to India, used to have to put up with guinea worms. But now people filter their drinking water, so they don't swallow any copepods with baby guinea worms inside. Simple as that. Guinea worm is now on its way to being an endangered species, all because of a little bit of knowledge.

Built-in Defence

Breaking the links in a parasite's life-cycle will eventually finish it off. But even without the help of knowledge or medicine, animals and humans have a built-in defence system to protect them against parasites that get inside their bodies. It's called the immune system, and in mammals like us humans, it works brilliantly well.

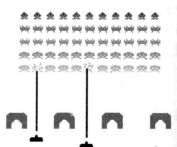

The immune system is made up of millions and millions of tiny cells that patrol all parts of your body like soldiers on the look-out for invaders, from big parasites like worms to tiny ones like plasmodia. These cells don't have eyes or ears, but they can recognize any parasite by the pattern of chemicals on its skin; then they attack. The immune cells can either mass together, dissolve the parasite's skin and eat it, or they can set up a fever, which makes the body so hot the parasite can't survive.

Parasites can get round the immune system by disguising themselves or changing so fast that the immune system doesn't recognize them, or by hiding inside a host's own cells – as plasmodium does. Most of the time the immune system wins, and you never even know about the invaders it has been fighting for you.

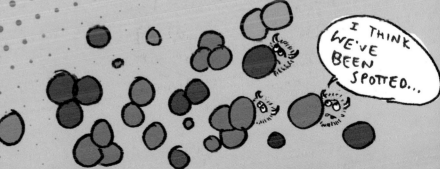

I'm Only Marrying You for Your Immune System...

Immune systems and parasites have been battling away in human bodies for many thousands of years. Right now, this minute, your immune system is fighting invaders you'll never even know about. Without your immune system you'd die. In fact, your immune system is so important that one day it might tell you who to marry!

Scientists finding out about how humans choose their mates found that people prefer partners with immune systems that have the bits that their own systems lack, so that any children they have together will be even better at fighting parasites.

But how do you know? Apparently someone with a complementary immune system just smells nice to you!

53

THE IMMUNE SYSTEM

A BIT THAT THE IMMUNE SYSTEM LACKS

Planet Parasite

I really wouldn't like you to go away with the idea that parasites are all bad, because as we humans find out more about them, we discover ways in which they can help us, not just harm us.

Some pests of crops can be controlled by parasites, so farmers don't have to use chemicals that might kill other wildlife too. Mealy bugs that were destroying cassava, the most important food crop in Africa, were killed off by bringing in a little wasp that is a parasite of mealy bugs.

Parasites can even cure diseases. Conditions like allergies and bowel disease can be helped by giving sufferers a controlled dose of parasitic worms. Although scientists are not yet sure why this works, it could be that humans actually *need* parasites. It certainly looks as if parasites are a vital part of nature – from whole habitats to single cells. Scientists studying tropical forests have found that plenty of parasites is a sign that a jungle is doing well. Almost every cell in every plant and animal contains tiny grains called mitochondria, that act like batteries, giving the cells energy. These mitochondria invaded the first cells millions of years ago as parasites, and became essential parts of every living thing.

LITTLE PARASITIC WASPS
URK!
MEALY BUGS IN AFRICA
WORM MEDICINE
A CELL
A CELL'S NUCLEUS
MITOCHONDRIA IN CELLS

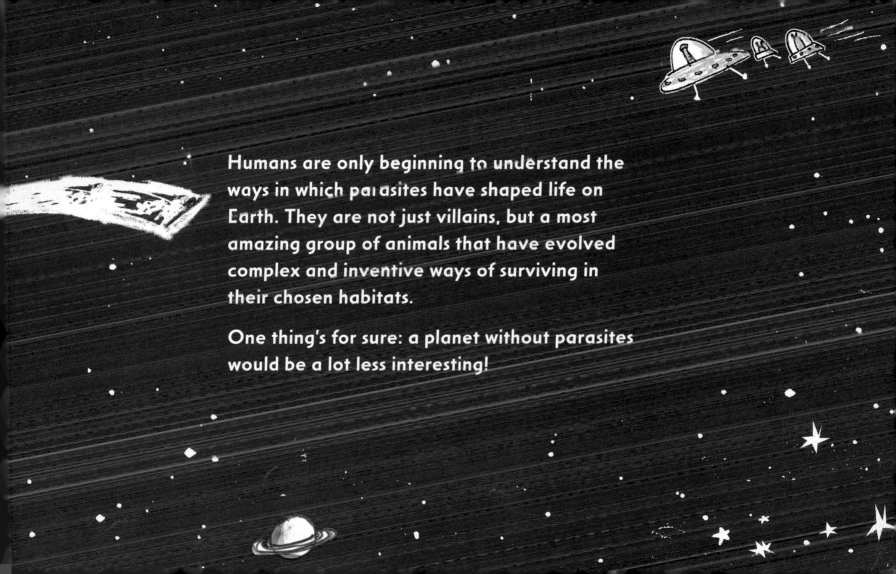

Humans are only beginning to understand the ways in which parasites have shaped life on Earth. They are not just villains, but a most amazing group of animals that have evolved complex and inventive ways of surviving in their chosen habitats.

One thing's for sure: a planet without parasites would be a lot less interesting!

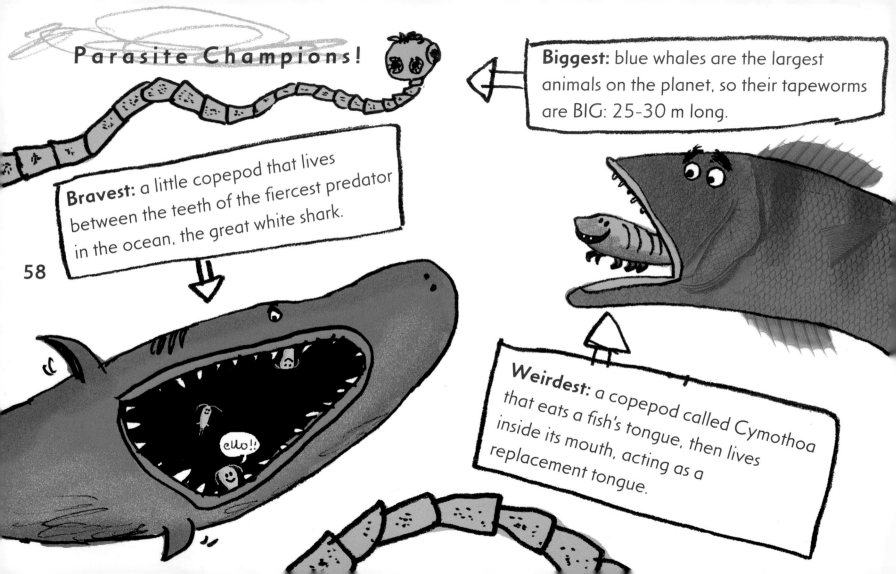

Parasite Champions!

Biggest: blue whales are the largest animals on the planet, so their tapeworms are BIG: 25-30 m long.

Bravest: a little copepod that lives between the teeth of the fiercest predator in the ocean, the great white shark.

58

ello!!

Weirdest: a copepod called Cymothoa that eats a fish's tongue, then lives inside its mouth, acting as a replacement tongue.

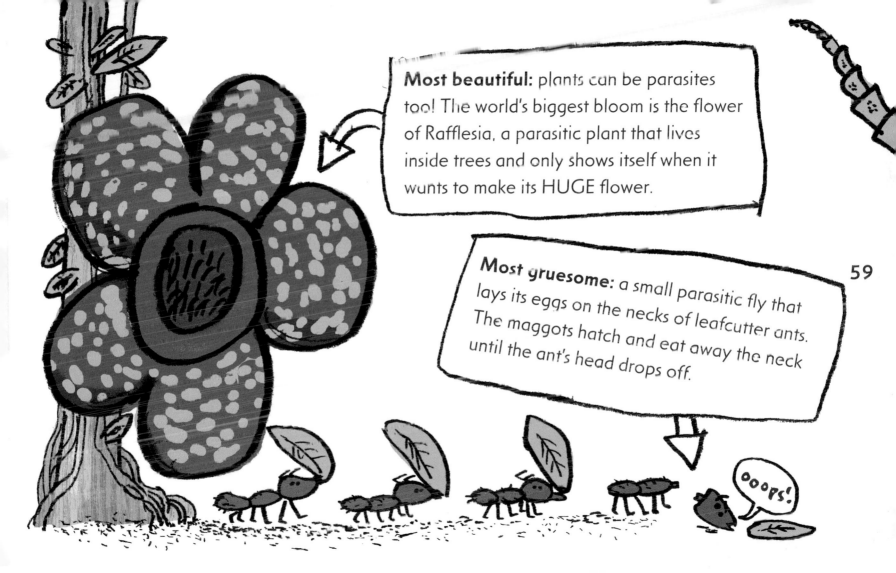

Most beautiful: plants can be parasites too! The world's biggest bloom is the flower of Rafflesia, a parasitic plant that lives inside trees and only shows itself when it wants to make its HUGE flower.

59

Most gruesome: a small parasitic fly that lays its eggs on the necks of leafcutter ants. The maggots hatch and eat away the neck until the ant's head drops off.

ooops!

INDEX

GLOSSARY

Ectoparasite – is a parasite that lives on the outside of a body (up noses and in ears still count as outside).

Endoparasite – is a parasite that lives inside a body, in the gut or organs or blood.

Habitat – is the sort of place where an animal or plant lives: gorillas' habitat is rainforest; the habitat of sidewinder snakes is desert.

Host – is the animal or plant that a parasite lives on or in, its habitat.

Immune system – millions of cells devoted to protecting a body from parasites large and teeny.

Invertebrate – an animal without a skeleton on the inside. Worms, insects, shrimps and squid are all invertebrates; fish, amphibians, reptiles, birds and mammals aren't.

Mitochondria – a tiny part of a cell that helps it to burn food and make energy for life.

Primary host – the host that the parasite breeds in.

Secondary host – the host that the parasite doesn't breed in.

Vertebrate – animals with skeletons on the inside: amphibians, reptiles, birds, mammals and fish.

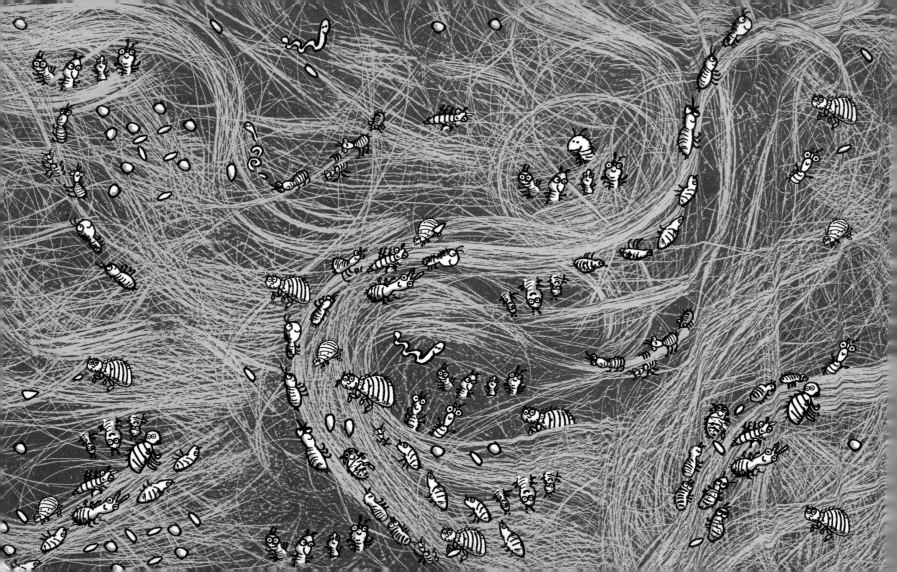